THIS JOURNAL BELONGS TO:

A BOY'S PRAYER JOURNAL
PB & J Prayers, Vol. 2

A Boy's PRAYER JOURNAL

PB & J *Prayers*

VOL. 2

Hi there!

Welcome to your new "PB & J" Prayer Journal. You are about to start a great adventure--of getting to know God better through prayer! But before you jump in, here are a few things to know before you start.

WHY USE A PRAYER JOURNAL?

If you hadn't eaten for a week, how would feel about a PB&J sandwich? I'll bet you'd be pretty excited about it, wouldnt you? Eating food fills up our stomachs and gives renewed energy for the day. It takes the hunger away so we can enjoy our life.

Just like your stomachs, your hearts can feel "hungry" too--you get hungry for God! You might notice yourself feeling worried, or crabby, or sad, or overwhelmed. Those are all signs that your heart is hungry: You need to fill up with God!

A lot of people just think of prayer as a chance to ask God for everything *they* want, and then they move on with their day. But that's like eating a bite of a sandwich, instead of enjoying the whole thing! It's not really enough to fill you up and give you the strength you need.

In addition to telling God the things you want, you can also use prayer to praise God and bless others. You can listen to God's Word and think about what *He* wants too.

> **DON'T SETTLE FOR LITTLE "BITES" OF PRAYER. TAKE TIME TO EAT A WHOLE PRAYER "SANDWICH" AND HAVE A DEEPER CONVERSATION WITH GOD!**

By adding these things to your prayers, you "fill up" your heart--with gratitude and trust and love. And this prayer journal can help you do that. So don't settle for little "bites" of prayer. Take time to eat a whole prayer "sandwich" and have a deeper conversation with God!

WHY PB & J?

There's no special formuala you have to use when you pray. God loves it when you talk to him, anywhere, anytime. The letters "PB & J" are just a little way to help you remember the different things you can talk to God about. Here's what they stand for:

> **There's no special formula you have to use when you pray. God loves it when you talk to him, anywhere, anytime!**

P IS FOR PRAISE & THANKS:

There are so many reasons to praise God. And he gives us so much to be thankful for! When you take time to give praise & thanks to God, you *fill your heart with gratitude and trust.*

B IS FOR BLESS OTHERS:

We might not have the power to fix everyone's problems--but God does! We can ask God to bless others and help them with their struggles. When you talk with God about the needs of others, you *fill your heart with compassion.*

J IS FOR JOIN WITH GOD:

What is *God* trying to say to *you*? God is always at work in your world and in your heart--and he wants to help you grow in your faith. When you ask God to help you join in that work, you *fill your heart with wisdom.*

HOW TO USE THIS JOURNAL

Each two-page spread in this prayer journal will give you a special prayer prompt and Bible verse to help you focus on "P" "B" or "J." You'll also find lots of writing spaces where you can share your thoughts and feelings with God. You can fill out both pages at a time, or divide it into smaller chunks for each day.

Prayer is, above all, a way to spend time with God. However you choose to fill these pages, know that **God is always delighted to spend time talking with you!**

READ "Can you bring forth the constellations in their seasons or lead out the Bear with its cubs? Do you know the laws of the heavens? Can you set up God's dominion over the earth?"

- Job 38:32-33

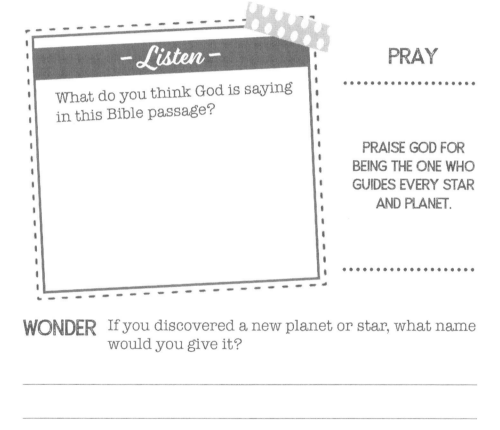

– Listen –

What do you think God is saying in this Bible passage?

PRAY

PRAISE GOD FOR BEING THE ONE WHO GUIDES EVERY STAR AND PLANET.

WONDER If you discovered a new planet or star, what name would you give it?

THANK-YOU FOR:

FORGIVE ME FOR:

People To Pray For

HELP ME TO SHOW LOVE TODAY BY:

On My Mind

Tell God about your worries and/or desires.

. . . .

God, I give all my worries, fears, and desires to you. Please help me to trust you today.

. . . .

P

READ "Seek the peace and prosperity of the city to which I have carried you into exile. Pray to the LORD for it, because if it prospers, you too will prosper."

- Jeremiah 29:7

— *Listen* —

What do you think God is saying in this Bible passage?

PRAY

PRAY FOR THE PEOPLE WHO WORK AT THE BUSINESSES IN YOUR COMMUNITY. ASK GOD TO GIVE THEM JOY IN THEIR WORK AND TO HELP YOUR COMMUNITY PROSPER.

WONDER What do you think is the best job someone could have? The worst job?

_____

_____

_____

_____

THANK-YOU FOR:

FORGIVE ME FOR:

Tell God about your
worries and/or desires.

People
To Pray For

HELP ME TO SHOW LOVE TODAY BY:

God, I give all my
worries, fears, and
desires to you.
Please help me to
trust you today.

B

READ "Finally, brothers and sisters, whatever is true, whatever is noble, whatever is right, whatever is pure, whatever is lovely, whatever is admirable—if anything is excellent or praiseworthy—think about such things."

- Philippians 4:8-9

- Listen -

What do you think God is saying in this Bible passage?

PRAY

ASK GOD TO GIVE YOU THE STRENGTH TO MAKE WISE CHOICES ABOUT ENTERTAINMENT.

WONDER What TV shows, movies, books, or video games do you enjoy? Do they give you good examples or bad examples to follow?

_____

_____

_____

_____

THANK-YOU FOR:

_____

_____

_____

_____

FORGIVE ME FOR:

_____

_____

_____

_____

People To Pray For

HELP ME TO SHOW LOVE TODAY BY:

_____

_____

On My Mind

Tell God about your worries and/or desires.

God, I give all my worries, fears, and desires to you. Please help me to trust you today.

J

– Praise –

READ "How good and pleasant it is when God's people live together in unity!"

- Pslam 133:1

– Listen –

What do you think God is saying in this Bible passage?

PRAY

· · · · · · · · · · · · · · · · · · ·

THANK GOD FOR YOUR FAMILY AND THE SPECIAL MOMENTS YOU HAVE SHARED.

· · · · · · · · · · · · · · · · · · ·

WONDER What do you enjoy doing with your family? What is one of your favorite family memories?

_____

_____

_____

_____

THANK-YOU FOR:

_____

_____

_____

_____

FORGIVE ME FOR:

_____

_____

_____

_____

People To Pray For

HELP ME TO SHOW LOVE TODAY BY:

_____

_____

On My Mind

Tell God about your worries and/or desires.

God, I give all my worries, fears, and desires to you. Please help me to trust you today.

P

Bless

READ "See, I have chosen Bezalel . . . and I have filled him with the Spirit of God, with wisdom, with understanding, with knowledge and with all kinds of skills—to make artistic designs."

- Exodus 31:2-4

— Listen —

What do you think God is saying in this Bible passage?

PRAY

PRAY FOR CHRISTIANS WHO CREATE ART (WRITERS, PAINTERS, MUSICIANS, ETC.) ASK GOD TO INSPIRE THEM TO SHOW HIS BEAUTY AND TRUTH THROUGH THEIR WORK.

WONDER Can you think of three ways your family enjoys the creative work of others?

THANK-YOU FOR:

_____
_____
_____
_____

FORGIVE ME FOR:

_____
_____
_____
_____

People To Pray For

HELP ME TO SHOW LOVE TODAY BY:

_____
_____

On My Mind

Tell God about your worries and/or desires.

. . . .

God, I give all my worries, fears, and desires to you. Please help me to trust you today.

. . . .

B

READ "The LORD is my light and my salvation—whom shall I fear? The LORD is the stronghold of my life—of whom shall I be afraid?"

- Psalm 27:1-2

— Listen —

What do you think God is saying in this Bible passage?

PRAY

ASK GOD TO GIVE YOU COURAGE WHEN YOU ARE SCARED AND TO REMEMBER THAT HE IS STRONGER THAN ANYTHING YOU FEAR.

WONDER What makes you feel afraid? What do you do when you feel scared?

_____

_____

_____

_____

THANK-YOU FOR:

_____

_____

_____

_____

FORGIVE ME FOR:

_____

_____

_____

_____

People To Pray For

HELP ME TO SHOW LOVE TODAY BY:

_____

_____

On My Mind

Tell God about your worries and/or desires.

God, I give all my worries, fears, and desires to you. Please help me to trust you today.

J

— Praise —

READ "You are worthy, our Lord and God, to receive glory and honor and power, for you created all things, and by your will they were created and have their being."

- Revelation 4:11

— Listen —

What do you think God is saying in this Bible passage?

PRAY

· · · · · · · · · · · · · · · · · · ·

THANK GOD FOR THE GIFT OF HIS AMAZING CREATION.

· · · · · · · · · · · · · · · · · · ·

WONDER What is your favorite animal? What is something beautiful you've seen in nature this week?

THANK-YOU FOR:

_____

_____

_____

_____

FORGIVE ME FOR:

_____

_____

_____

_____

People To Pray For

HELP ME TO SHOW LOVE TODAY BY:

_____

_____

On My Mind

Tell God about your worries and/or desires.

• • • • • • • • • • • • • • • • • • •

God, I give all my worries, fears, and desires to you. Please help me to trust you today.

• • • • • • • • • • • • • • • • • • •

READ   "Let us not become weary in doing good, for at the proper time we will reap a harvest if we do not give up."

- Galatians 6:9

— *Listen* —

What do you think God is saying in this Bible passage?

PRAY

PRAY FOR THE VOLUNTEERS IN YOUR COMMUNITY. ASK GOD TO ENCOURAGE THEM AND GIVE THEM STRENGTH FOR THEIR WORK.

WONDER   Do you know someone who volunteers time to help people in need? What kind of work do they do?

THANK-YOU FOR:

_____

_____

_____

_____

FORGIVE ME FOR:

_____

_____

_____

_____

People To Pray For

HELP ME TO SHOW LOVE TODAY BY:

_____

_____

On My Mind

Tell God about your worries and/or desires.

· · · · · · · · · · · · · · · · · · · ·

God, I give all my worries, fears, and desires to you. Please help me to trust you today.

· · · · · · · · · · · · · · · · · · · ·

READ "It is better to take refuge in the Lord than to trust in people."

- Psalm 118:8 (NLT)

"Some trust in chariots and some in horses, but we trust in the name of the LORD our God."

- Psalm 20:7

- Listen -

What do you think God is saying in this Bible passage?

PRAY

ASK GOD TO HELP YOU PUT YOUR TRUST IN HIM ALONE.

WONDER What are some things that people put their trust in, besides God?

THANK-YOU FOR:

_____

_____

_____

_____

FORGIVE ME FOR:

_____

_____

_____

_____

Tell God about your
worries and/or desires.

*People
To Pray For*

God, I give all my
worries, fears, and
desires to you.
Please help me to
trust you today.

HELP ME TO SHOW LOVE TODAY BY:

_____

_____

J

READ   "And we know that in all things God works for the good of those who love him, who have been called according to his purpose."

- Romans 8:28

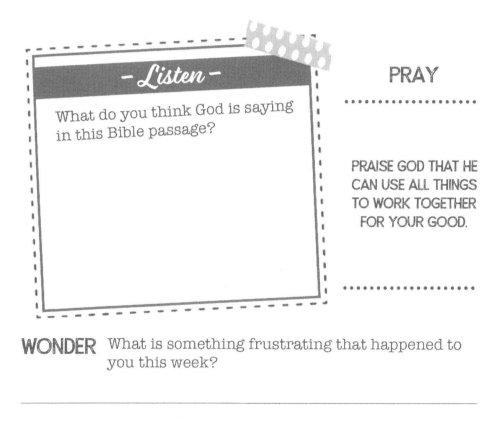

– Listen –

What do you think God is saying in this Bible passage?

PRAY

. . . .

PRAISE GOD THAT HE CAN USE ALL THINGS TO WORK TOGETHER FOR YOUR GOOD.

. . . .

WONDER   What is something frustrating that happened to you this week?

THANK-YOU FOR:

_____

_____

_____

_____

FORGIVE ME FOR:

_____

_____

_____

_____

People To Pray For

HELP ME TO SHOW LOVE TODAY BY:

_____

_____

On My Mind

Tell God about your worries and/or desires.

• • • • • • • • • • • • • • • • • • • •

God, I give all my worries, fears, and desires to you. Please help me to trust you today.

• • • • • • • • • • • • • • • • • • • •

READ "Continue to remember those in prison as if you were together with them in prison, and those who are mistreated as if you yourselves were suffering."

- Hebrews 13:3

— *Listen* —

What do you think God is saying in this Bible passage?

PRAY

PRAY FOR CHRISTIANS WHO GET PERSECUTED OR PUT IN PRISON FOR THEIR FAITH. ASK GOD TO KEEP THEIR FAITH STRONG AND TO HELP HIS CHURCH CONTINUE TO GROW IN THE WORLD.

WONDER What would be different about your life if it was illegal to be a Christian in your country?

_____

_____

_____

_____

THANK-YOU FOR:

_____

_____

_____

_____

FORGIVE ME FOR:

_____

_____

_____

_____

People To Pray For

HELP ME TO SHOW LOVE TODAY BY:

_____

_____

On My Mind

Tell God about your worries and/or desires.

· · · · · · · · · · · · · · · · · · · ·

God, I give all my worries, fears, and desires to you. Please help me to trust you today.

· · · · · · · · · · · · · · · · · · · ·

B

READ "Cast all your anxiety on him because he cares for you."

- 1 Peter 5:7

"Can any one of you by worrying add a single hour to your life?"

- Matthew 6:27

— Listen —

What do you think God is saying in this Bible passage?

PRAY

ASK GOD TO HELP YOU LEAVE YOUR WORRIES TO HIM AND TRUST THAT HE WILL TAKE GOOD CARE OF YOU.

WONDER Do you ever worry that something bad might happen? Or that something good *won't* happen?

THANK-YOU FOR:

_____

_____

_____

_____

FORGIVE ME FOR:

_____

_____

_____

_____

People To Pray For

HELP ME TO SHOW LOVE TODAY BY:

_____

_____

On My Mind

Tell God about your worries and/or desires.

God, I give all my worries, fears, and desires to you. Please help me to trust you today.

J

– Praise –

READ "As long as the earth endures, seedtime and harvest, cold and heat, summer and winter, day and night will never cease."

- Genesis 8:22

– Listen –

What do you think God is saying in this Bible passage?

PRAY

· · · · · · · · · · · · · · · · · · · ·

PRAISE GOD FOR SENDING THE SEASONS EVERY YEAR, AND THE WAY THEY REMIND US OF HIS FAITHFULNESS.

· · · · · · · · · · · · · · · · · · · ·

WONDER What is your favorite season of the year? Why do you like it?

_____

_____

_____

_____

THANK-YOU FOR:

_____

_____

_____

_____

FORGIVE ME FOR:

_____

_____

_____

_____

People To Pray For

HELP ME TO SHOW LOVE TODAY BY:

_____

_____

On My Mind

Tell God about your worries and/or desires.

· · · · · · · · · · · · · · · · · · · ·

God, I give all my worries, fears, and desires to you. Please help me to trust you today.

· · · · · · · · · · · · · · · · · · · ·

READ " 'Truly I tell you, anyone who will not receive the kingdom of God like a little child will never enter it.' And [Jesus] took the children in his arms, placed his hands on them and blessed them."

- Mark 10:15-16

– Listen –

What do you think God is saying in this Bible passage?

PRAY

PRAY FOR ALL THE NEW BABIES WHO CAME INTO THE WORLD TODAY–AND THE PARENTS WHO WILL RAISE THEM.

WONDER Can you think of a Bible story that involves a baby or a child? How did Jesus feel about children?

THANK-YOU FOR:

_____

_____

_____

_____

FORGIVE ME FOR:

_____

_____

_____

_____

People To Pray For

HELP ME TO SHOW LOVE TODAY BY:

_____

_____

READ "I praise you because I am fearfully and wonderfully made; your works are wonderful, I know that full well."

- Psalm 139:14

— *Listen* —

What do you think God is saying in this Bible passage?

PRAY

ASK GOD TO HELP YOU BE CONFIDENT AND THANKFUL FOR THE UNIQUE PERSON HE CREATED YOU TO BE.

WONDER Do you ever wish that you had someone else's looks, or talents, or personality? What is something that is special about *you*?

THANK-YOU FOR:

_____

_____

_____

_____

FORGIVE ME FOR:

_____

_____

_____

_____

People To Pray For

HELP ME TO SHOW LOVE TODAY BY:

_____

_____

On My Mind

Tell God about your worries and/or desires.

God, I give all my worries, fears, and desires to you. Please help me to trust you today.

J

– Praise –

READ "Yours, LORD, is the greatness and the power and the glory and the majesty and the splendor, for everything in heaven and earth is yours. . . Wealth and honor come from you; you are the ruler of all things."

- 1 Chronicles 29:11-12

– Listen –

What do you think God is saying in this Bible passage?

PRAY

....

PRAISE GOD FOR BEING THE ONE WHO OWNS EVERYTHING IN HEAVEN AND EARTH.

....

WONDER If you could pick three new things to own right now, what would they be?

_____

_____

_____

_____

THANK-YOU FOR:

FORGIVE ME FOR:

People To Pray For

HELP ME TO SHOW LOVE TODAY BY:

On My Mind

Tell God about your worries and/or desires.

God, I give all my worries, fears, and desires to you. Please help me to trust you today.

READ "In everything set them an example by doing what is good. In your teaching show integrity, seriousness and soundness of speech that cannot be condemned."

- Titus 2:7-8

— Listen —

What do you think God is saying in this Bible passage?

PRAY

PRAY FOR CHRISTIAN TEACHERS AND PROFESSORS. ASK GOD TO GIVE THEM OPPORTUNITIES TO SHARE HIS TRUTH AS THEY TEACH THEIR STUDENTS.

WONDER If you were a teacher, what age and subject would you like to teach?

THANK-YOU FOR:

_____

_____

_____

_____

FORGIVE ME FOR:

_____

_____

_____

_____

People To Pray For

HELP ME TO SHOW LOVE TODAY BY:

_____

_____

On My Mind

Tell God about your worries and/or desires.

God, I give all my worries, fears, and desires to you. Please help me to trust you today.

READ "Work willingly at whatever you do, as though you were working for the Lord rather than for people."

- Colossians 3:23 (NLT)

— *Listen* —

What do you think God is saying in this Bible passage?

PRAY

ASK GOD TO GIVE YOU A GOOD ATTITUDE TOWARD LEARNING AND TO GIVE YOUR BEST EFFORT.

WONDER What parts of schoolwork do you enjoy? What parts are hard for you?

_____

_____

_____

_____

THANK-YOU FOR:

FORGIVE ME FOR:

Tell God about your
worries and/or desires.

*People
To Pray For*

God, I give all my
worries, fears, and
desires to you.
Please help me to
trust you today.

HELP ME TO SHOW LOVE TODAY BY:

J

READ   "For even the Son of Man did not come to be
served, but to serve, and to give his life as a
ransom for many."

- Mark 10:45

– Listen –

What do you think God is saying
in this Bible passage?

PRAY

PRAISE JESUS FOR
SHOWING YOU HOW
TO SERVE, EVEN TO
THE POINT OF GIVING
UP HIS LIFE FOR YOU.

WONDER   Can you name three different ways that Jesus
served other people?

_____

_____

_____

_____

THANK-YOU FOR:

_____

_____

_____

_____

FORGIVE ME FOR:

_____

_____

_____

_____

People To Pray For

HELP ME TO SHOW LOVE TODAY BY:

_____

_____

On My Mind

Tell God about your worries and/or desires.

• • • • • • • • • • • • • • • • • •

God, I give all my worries, fears, and desires to you. Please help me to trust you today.

• • • • • • • • • • • • • • • • • •

Bless

READ "The LORD is close to the brokenhearted and saves those who are crushed in spirit."

- Psalm 34:18

Listen

What do you think God is saying in this Bible passage?

PRAY

PRAY FOR SOMEONE WHO HAS LOST A PARENT, SPOUSE, OR CHILD IN THE LAST YEAR. ASK GOD TO BE CLOSE TO THEM AND COMFORT THEM IN THEIR GRIEF.

WONDER How can you encourage or help someone when they feel sad?

THANK-YOU FOR:

_____

_____

_____

_____

FORGIVE ME FOR:

_____

_____

_____

_____

People To Pray For

HELP ME TO SHOW LOVE TODAY BY:

_____

_____

On My Mind

Tell God about your worries and/or desires.

· · · · · · · · · · · · · · · · · · · ·

God, I give all my worries, fears, and desires to you. Please help me to trust you today.

· · · · · · · · · · · · · · · · · · · ·

B

READ "The righteous choose their friends carefully, but the way of the wicked leads them astray."

- Proverbs 12:26

— Listen —

What do you think God is saying in this Bible passage?

PRAY

· · · · · · · · · · · · · · · · · · ·

ASK GOD TO HELP YOU BE A GOOD INFLUENCE ON YOUR FRIENDS, AND TO CHOOSE FRIENDS WISELY.

· · · · · · · · · · · · · · · · · · ·

WONDER Do your friends help you make good choices? Or do they pull you toward bad choices?

THANK-YOU FOR:

_____

_____

_____

_____

FORGIVE ME FOR:

_____

_____

_____

_____

People To Pray For

HELP ME TO SHOW LOVE TODAY BY:

_____

_____

On My Mind

Tell God about your worries and/or desires.

God, I give all my worries, fears, and desires to you. Please help me to trust you today.

J

READ "I know that the LORD secures justice for the poor and upholds the cause of the needy."

- Psalm 140:12

– Listen –

What do you think God is saying in this Bible passage?

PRAY

PRAISE GOD FOR CARING ABOUT JUSTICE AND FOR CARING FOR THE POOR.

WONDER If you could do three things to help poor people in our world, what would you choose to do?

THANK-YOU FOR:

_____

_____

_____

_____

FORGIVE ME FOR:

_____

_____

_____

_____

People To Pray For

HELP ME TO SHOW LOVE TODAY BY:

_____

_____

On My Mind

Tell God about your worries and/or desires.

. . . .

God, I give all my worries, fears, and desires to you. Please help me to trust you today.

. . . .

READ "The king said to Daniel, 'Surely your God is the God of gods and the Lord of kings and a revealer of mysteries, for you were able to reveal this mystery.' "

- Daniel 2:47

— Listen —

What do you think God is saying in this Bible passage?

PRAY

PRAY FOR THE SCIENTISTS AND RESEARCHERS WHO ARE WORKING TO FIGHT DISEASE. ASK GOD TO REVEAL MYSTERIES TO THEM THAT LEAD TO NEW TECHNOLOGIES AND MEDICINES.

WONDER If you could pick one medical problem to cure today, which one would you pick?

THANK-YOU FOR:

_____

_____

_____

_____

FORGIVE ME FOR:

_____

_____

_____

_____

People To Pray For

HELP ME TO SHOW LOVE TODAY BY:

_____

_____

On My Mind

Tell God about your worries and/or desires.

God, I give all my worries, fears, and desires to you. Please help me to trust you today.

B

READ "Listen to advice and accept discipline, and at the end you will be counted among the wise."

- Proverbs 19:20

- *Listen* -

What do you think God is saying in this Bible passage?

PRAY

. . . .

ASK GOD TO HELP YOU ACCEPT DISCIPLINE WHEN IT HAPPENS SO THAT YOU CAN LEARN FROM IT AND DO BETTER NEXT TIME.

. . . .

WONDER When is the last time you were punished, or given a word of caution? What did you learn from the experience?

_____

_____

_____

_____

THANK-YOU FOR:

_____

_____

_____

_____

FORGIVE ME FOR:

_____

_____

_____

_____

People To Pray For

HELP ME TO SHOW LOVE TODAY BY:

_____

_____

On My Mind

Tell God about your worries and/or desires.

• • • • • • • • • • • • • • • • • • •

God, I give all my worries, fears, and desires to you. Please help me to trust you today.

• • • • • • • • • • • • • • • • • • •

J

– Praise –

READ "If we are unfaithful, he remains faithful, for he cannot deny who he is."

– 2 Timothy 2:13 (NLT)

– Listen –

What do you think God is saying in this Bible passage?

PRAY

PRAISE GOD FOR STAYING FAITHFUL TO US, EVEN WHEN WE DON'T ALWAYS STAY FAITHFUL TO HIM.

WONDER Can you think of a Bible character who sinned badly, but who was still loved by God?

THANK-YOU FOR:

_____
_____
_____
_____

FORGIVE ME FOR:

_____
_____
_____
_____

People To Pray For

HELP ME TO SHOW LOVE TODAY BY:

_____
_____

On My Mind

Tell God about your worries and/or desires.

. . . .

God, I give all my worries, fears, and desires to you. Please help me to trust you today.

. . . .

— Bless —

READ   "Ask the Lord of the harvest, therefore, to send out workers into his harvest field."

- Matthew 9:38

— Listen —

What do you think God is saying in this Bible passage?

PRAY

PRAY FOR ALL THOSE WHO DON'T BELIEVE IN GOD: ASK GOD TO RAISE UP MORE WORKERS WHO WILL MEET THEIR NEEDS AND TEACH THEM ABOUT JESUS.

WONDER   Why do you think some people do not believe in God? What might help them believe?

_____

_____

_____

_____

THANK-YOU FOR:

_____

_____
_____
_____
_____

FORGIVE ME FOR:

_____
_____
_____
_____
_____

People To Pray For

HELP ME TO SHOW LOVE TODAY BY:

_____
_____

On My Mind

Tell God about your worries and/or desires.

· · · · · · · · · · · · · · · · · · ·

God, I give all my worries, fears, and desires to you. Please help me to trust you today.

· · · · · · · · · · · · · · · · · · ·

B

READ "If you need wisdom, ask our generous God, and he will give it to you. He will not rebuke you for asking."

- James 1:5 (NLT)

- Listen -

What do you think God is saying in this Bible passage?

PRAY

ASK GOD TO HELP YOU TURN TO HIM FOR WISDOM WHEN CONFUSING SITUATIONS HAPPEN.

WONDER Can you think of a time when you felt confused about the right thing to do? What can you do when you feel confused?

THANK-YOU FOR:

_____
_____
_____
_____

FORGIVE ME FOR:

_____
_____
_____
_____

On My Mind

Tell God about your worries and/or desires.

People To Pray For

God, I give all my worries, fears, and desires to you. Please help me to trust you today.

HELP ME TO SHOW LOVE TODAY BY:

_____
_____

J

READ "The LORD is gracious and compassionate, slow to anger and rich in love. The Lord is good to all; he has compassion on all he has made."

- Psalm 145:8-9

– Listen –

What do you think God is saying in this Bible passage?

PRAY

· · · · · · · · · · · · · · · · · · · ·

PRAISE GOD THAT HE IS COMPASSIONATE TOWARD YOU AND SLOW TO ANGER.

· · · · · · · · · · · · · · · · · · · ·

WONDER What kind of situations make you feel angry? How do you react when you are angry?

_____

_____

_____

_____

THANK-YOU FOR:

_____

_____

_____

_____

FORGIVE ME FOR:

_____

_____

_____

_____

People To Pray For

HELP ME TO SHOW LOVE TODAY BY:

_____

_____

On My Mind

Tell God about your worries and/or desires.

· · · · · · · · · · · · · · · · · · · ·

God, I give all my worries, fears, and desires to you. Please help me to trust you today.

· · · · · · · · · · · · · · · · · · · ·

— Bless —

READ "May God, who gives this patience and encouragement, help you live in complete harmony with each other, as is fitting for followers of Christ Jesus. Then all of you can join together with one voice, giving praise and glory to God, the Father of our Lord Jesus Christ."

- Romans 15:5-6 (NLT)

— Listen —

What do you think God is saying in this Bible passage?

PRAY

PRAY FOR A COUPLE THAT HAS RECENTLY BEEN MARRIED. ASK GOD TO HELP THEM LIVE IN HARMONY AND CREATE A UNIFIED FAMILY.

WONDER Would you like to get married someday? Why or why not?

_____

_____

_____

_____

THANK-YOU FOR:

_____

_____

_____

_____

FORGIVE ME FOR:

_____

_____

_____

_____

People To Pray For

HELP ME TO SHOW LOVE TODAY BY:

_____

_____

On My Mind

Tell God about your worries and/or desires.

God, I give all my worries, fears, and desires to you. Please help me to trust you today.

READ "Always be humble and gentle. Be patient with each other, making allowance for each other's faults because of your love."

- Ephesians 4:2 (NLT)

– *Listen* –

What do you think God is saying in this Bible passage?

PRAY

ASK GOD TO GIVE YOU PATIENCE WITH THE FAULTS OF OTHERS AND A GOOD ATTITUDE WHEN YOU HAVE TO WAIT.

WONDER How do you react when you have to wait for others? How do you react when they make a mistake?

_____

_____

_____

_____

THANK-YOU FOR:

_____

_____

_____

_____

FORGIVE ME FOR:

_____

_____

_____

_____

People To Pray For

HELP ME TO SHOW LOVE TODAY BY:

_____

_____

On My Mind

Tell God about your worries and/or desires.

God, I give all my worries, fears, and desires to you. Please help me to trust you today.

J

– Praise –

READ "Do you not know? Have you not heard? The LORD is the everlasting God, the Creator of the ends of the earth. He will not grow tired or weary, and his understanding no one can fathom. He gives strength to the weary . . ."

- Isaiah 40:28-29

– Listen –

What do you think God is saying in this Bible passage?

PRAY

· · · · · · · · · · · · · · · · · · ·

PRAISE GOD BECAUSE HE NEVER GROWS TIRED AND HE GIVES YOU STRENGTH WHEN YOU NEED IT.

· · · · · · · · · · · · · · · · · · ·

WONDER Can you remember a time when you felt really tired or overwhelmed? What happened?

_____

_____

_____

_____

THANK-YOU FOR:

_____

_____

_____

_____

FORGIVE ME FOR:

_____

_____

_____

_____

_____

People To Pray For

On My Mind

Tell God about your worries and/or desires.

God, I give all my worries, fears, and desires to you. Please help me to trust you today.

HELP ME TO SHOW LOVE TODAY BY:

_____

_____

P

READ "God is our refuge and strength, an ever-present help in trouble. Therefore we will not fear."

- Psalm 46:1-2

– *Listen* –

What do you think God is saying in this Bible passage?

PRAY

PRAY FOR THE MEN AND WOMEN SERVING IN THE MILITARY AND THEIR FAMILIES BACK HOME. ASK GOD TO GIVE THEM COURAGE AND TO KNOW HE IS WITH THEM.

WONDER What would you miss the most about your home if you were a soldier serving overseas?

THANK-YOU FOR:

_____

_____

_____

_____

_____

FORGIVE ME FOR:

_____

_____

_____

_____

_____

People
To Pray For

HELP ME TO SHOW LOVE TODAY BY:

_____

_____

On My Mind

Tell God about your worries and/or desires.

· · · · · · · · · · · · · · · · · · ·

God, I give all my worries, fears, and desires to you. Please help me to trust you today.

· · · · · · · · · · · · · · · · · · ·

READ "For we are God's handiwork, created in Christ Jesus to do good works, which God prepared in advance for us to do."

- Ephesians 2:10

- Listen -

What do you think God is saying in this Bible passage?

PRAY

ASK GOD TO HELP YOU SEE THE UNIQUE PURPOSE HE HAS FOR YOU BOTH RIGHT NOW, AND AS YOU GROW.

WONDER What kind of activities do you enjoy? How could you use them to bless others?

THANK-YOU FOR:

_____

_____

_____

_____

FORGIVE ME FOR:

_____

_____

_____

_____

People To Pray For

HELP ME TO SHOW LOVE TODAY BY:

_____

_____

On My Mind

Tell God about your worries and/or desires.

. . . .

God, I give all my worries, fears, and desires to you. Please help me to trust you today.

. . . .

J

READ "Oh, how great are God's riches and wisdom and knowledge! How impossible it is for us to understand his decisions and his ways!"

- Romans 11:33 (NLT)

— *Listen* —

What do you think God is saying in this Bible passage?

PRAY

PRAISE GOD FOR KNOWING ALL THINGS, AND HAVING FAR GREATER WISDOM AND UNDERSTANDING THAN WE DO.

WONDER What is something about the world that you would like to learn more about?

THANK-YOU FOR:

_____

_____

_____

_____

FORGIVE ME FOR:

_____

_____

_____

_____

People To Pray For

HELP ME TO SHOW LOVE TODAY BY:

_____

_____

On My Mind

Tell God about your worries and/or desires.

God, I give all my worries, fears, and desires to you. Please help me to trust you today.

READ "Rejoice with those who rejoice; mourn with those who mourn. Live in harmony with one another."

- Romans 12:15-16

- Listen -

What do you think God is saying in this Bible passage?

PRAY

PRAY FOR SOMEONE WHO IS CELEBRATING SOMETHING SPECIAL RIGHT NOW. (A NEW JOB, A VACATION, A NEW HOUSE, ETC.) THANK GOD FOR HIS GOODNESS AND CELEBRATE WITH THEM.

WONDER What is one of the best things that happened to you this week?

THANK-YOU FOR:

Tell God about your
worries and/or desires.

FORGIVE ME FOR:

People
To Pray For

God, I give all my
worries, fears, and
desires to you.
Please help me to
trust you today.

HELP ME TO SHOW LOVE TODAY BY:

READ "Keep this Book of the Law always on your lips; meditate on it day and night, so that you may be careful to do everything written in it. Then you will be prosperous and successful."

- Joshua 1:8

- Listen -

What do you think God is saying in this Bible passage?

PRAY

ASK GOD TO GIVE YOU A HUNGER FOR STUDYING THE BIBLE, SO THAT YOU CAN GROW CLOSER TO HIM.

WONDER What are some benefits from reading the Bible? How often do you read God's Word?

THANK-YOU FOR:

_____

_____

_____

_____

FORGIVE ME FOR:

_____

_____

_____

_____

*People
To Pray For*

HELP ME TO SHOW LOVE TODAY BY:

_____

_____

On My Mind

Tell God about your
worries and/or desires.

God, I give all my
worries, fears, and
desires to you.
Please help me to
trust you today.

READ "He will yet fill your mouth with laughter and your lips with shouts of joy."

- Job 8:21

— *Listen* —

What do you think God is saying in this Bible passage?

PRAY

· · · · · · · · · · · · · · · · · · · ·

THANK GOD FOR
GIVING YOU THE
ABILITY TO LAUGH
AND FEEL JOY.

· · · · · · · · · · · · · · · · · · · ·

WONDER What is something that gives you joy? And what makes you laugh?

THANK-YOU FOR:

_____

_____

_____

_____

FORGIVE ME FOR:

_____

_____

_____

_____

People
To Pray For

HELP ME TO SHOW LOVE TODAY BY:

_____

_____

On My Mind

Tell God about your worries and/or desires.

· · · · · · · · · · · · · · · ·

God, I give all my worries, fears, and desires to you. Please help me to trust you today.

· · · · · · · · · · · · · · · ·

READ "Whoever oppresses the poor shows contempt for their Maker, but whoever is kind to the needy honors God."

- Proverbs 14:31

— *Listen* —

What do you think God is saying in this Bible passage?

PRAY

PRAY FOR PEOPLE IN YOUR COMMUNITY WHO ARE HOMELESS. ASK GOD TO PROTECT THEM FROM HARM AND TO LEAD THEM TO PEOPLE WHO CAN HELP THEM FIND A HOME.

WONDER What are three things you like about the house you live in?

THANK-YOU FOR:

_____

_____
_____
_____
_____

FORGIVE ME FOR:

_____
_____
_____
_____

People To Pray For

God, I give all my worries, fears, and desires to you. Please help me to trust you today.

HELP ME TO SHOW LOVE TODAY BY:

_____
_____

READ "But grow in the grace and knowledge of our Lord and Savior Jesus Christ. To him be glory both now and forever!"

- 2 Peter 3:18

- Listen -

What do you think God is saying in this Bible passage?

PRAY

ASK GOD TO HELP YOU PAY ATTENTION AND LEARN FROM THE TEACHING OPPORTUNITIES YOU HAVE AT CHURCH.

WONDER What is something new you have learned recently from a sermon or Sunday school class?

_____

_____

_____

_____

THANK-YOU FOR:

_____

_____

_____

_____

FORGIVE ME FOR:

_____

_____

_____

_____

_____

People To Pray For

HELP ME TO SHOW LOVE TODAY BY:

_____

_____

On My Mind

Tell God about your worries and/or desires.

God, I give all my worries, fears, and desires to you. Please help me to trust you today.

J

READ "If I go up to the heavens, you are there; if I make my bed in the depths, you are there. If I rise on the wings of the dawn, if I settle on the far side of the sea, even there your hand will guide me, your right hand will hold me fast."

- Pslam 139:8-10

– *Listen* –

What do you think God is saying in this Bible passage?

PRAY

PRAISE GOD FOR GIVING YOU HIS SPIRIT, WHICH WILL ALWAYS BE WITH YOU AND GUIDE YOU, WHEREVER YOU GO.

WONDER If you could travel to any place in the world, where would you visit? What would you do there?

_____

_____

_____

_____

THANK-YOU FOR:

_____

_____

_____

_____

FORGIVE ME FOR:

_____

_____

_____

_____

*People
To Pray For*

HELP ME TO SHOW LOVE TODAY BY:

_____

_____

On My Mind

Tell God about your
worries and/or desires.

God, I give all my
worries, fears, and
desires to you.
Please help me to
trust you today.

— Bless —

READ "Remember your leaders, who spoke the word of God to you. Consider the outcome of their way of life and imitate their faith."

- Hebrews 13:7

— Listen —

What do you think God is saying in this Bible passage?

PRAY

PRAY FOR YOUR CHURCH AND ITS LEADERS. ASK GOD TO HELP THEM GROW IN FAITH AND WISDOM AS THEY LEAD AND TEACH YOUR CHURCH.

WONDER What is your favorite thing about your church community?

THANK-YOU FOR:

_____

_____

_____

_____

FORGIVE ME FOR:

_____

_____

_____

_____

People To Pray For

HELP ME TO SHOW LOVE TODAY BY:

_____

_____

On My Mind

Tell God about your worries and/or desires.

God, I give all my worries, fears, and desires to you. Please help me to trust you today.

— Join —

READ "Therefore, as God's chosen people, holy and dearly loved, clothe yourselves with compassion, kindness, humility, gentleness and patience."

- Colossians 3:12

— Listen —

What do you think God is saying in this Bible passage?

PRAY

ASK GOD TO HELP YOU PUT ON A GOOD ATTITUDE EVERY MORNING AND TO KEEP IT THROUGHOUT YOUR DAY.

WONDER What is one of your favorite pieces of clothing to wear? Why do you like it so much?

_____

_____

_____

_____

THANK-YOU FOR:

FORGIVE ME FOR:

People To Pray For

HELP ME TO SHOW LOVE TODAY BY:

On My Mind

Tell God about your worries and/or desires.

God, I give all my worries, fears, and desires to you. Please help me to trust you today.

J

READ "So you see, just as death came into the world through a man, now the resurrection from the dead has begun through another man. Just as everyone dies because we all belong to Adam, everyone who belongs to Christ will be given new life." - 1 Corinthians 15:21-22 (NLT)

– Listen –

What do you think God is saying in this Bible passage?

PRAY

PRAISE JESUS FOR OVERCOMING DEATH AND GIVING US THE GIFT OF ETERNAL LIFE!

WONDER If you could pick one person from history to come back to life and eat dinner with you, who would you pick?

THANK-YOU FOR:

_____

_____

_____

_____

FORGIVE ME FOR:

_____

_____

_____

_____

People To Pray For

HELP ME TO SHOW LOVE TODAY BY:

_____

_____

On My Mind

Tell God about your worries and/or desires.

· · · · · · · · · · · · · · · · · · ·

God, I give all my worries, fears, and desires to you. Please help me to trust you today.

· · · · · · · · · · · · · · · · · · ·

— Bless —

READ "In the same way, let your light shine before others, that they may see your good deeds and glorify your Father in heaven."

- Matthew 5:16

— Listen —

What do you think God is saying in this Bible passage?

PRAY

PRAY FOR A CHRISTIAN CELEBRITY. ASK GOD TO HELP THEM STAY FAITHFUL AND TO SHARE THE TRUTH ABOUT GOD WITH THE MANY PEOPLE WHO LOOK UP TO THEM.

WONDER If you became a famous celebrity, what would you want to be famous for?

_____

_____

_____

_____

THANK-YOU FOR:

_____

_____

_____

_____

FORGIVE ME FOR:

_____

_____

_____

_____

People To Pray For

HELP ME TO SHOW LOVE TODAY BY:

_____

_____

On My Mind

Tell God about your worries and/or desires.

· · · · · · · · · · · · · · · · · · · ·

God, I give all my worries, fears, and desires to you. Please help me to trust you today.

· · · · · · · · · · · · · · · · · · · ·

READ "Consider it pure joy, my brothers and sisters, whenever you face trials of many kinds, because you know that the testing of your faith produces perseverance. Let perseverance finish its work so that you may be mature and complete."

- James 1:2-4

— *Listen* —

What do you think God is saying in this Bible passage?

PRAY

ASK GOD TO GIVE YOU PERSEVERANCE SO THAT YOU WILL NOT GIVE UP WHEN YOU FACE FUTURE CHALLENGES.

WONDER What is one of the hardest tasks you have ever had to do? What helped you get through it?

THANK-YOU FOR:

_____

_____

_____

_____

FORGIVE ME FOR:

_____

_____

_____

_____

People To Pray For

HELP ME TO SHOW LOVE TODAY BY:

_____

_____

On My Mind

Tell God about your worries and/or desires.

God, I give all my worries, fears, and desires to you. Please help me to trust you today.

J

READ   "And my God will meet all your needs according to the riches of his glory in Christ Jesus. To our God and Father be glory for ever and ever. Amen."

- Philippians 4:19-20

– Listen –

What do you think God is saying in this Bible passage?

PRAY

PRAISE GOD FOR TAKING CARE OF ALL YOUR NEEDS, AND SOMETIMES GIVING YOU EVEN MORE THAN YOU ASK FOR.

WONDER   What are three needs God provided for you today?

THANK-YOU FOR:

_____

_____

_____

_____

FORGIVE ME FOR:

_____

_____

_____

_____

People To Pray For

HELP ME TO SHOW LOVE TODAY BY:

_____

_____

On My Mind

Tell God about your worries and/or desires.

. . . .

God, I give all my worries, fears, and desires to you. Please help me to trust you today.

. . . .

READ "The LORD hears the needy and does not despise his captive people."

- Psalm 69:33

— *Listen* —

What do you think God is saying in this Bible passage?

PRAY

PRAY FOR PRISONERS IN YOUR COUNTRY. ASK GOD TO GIVE THEM OPPORTUNITIES TO LEARN ABOUT HIS LOVE AND PROVIDE WAYS FOR THEM TO REBUILD THEIR LIVES.

WONDER How many people in the Bible can you think of who spent time in prison or jail?

THANK-YOU FOR:

_____

_____

_____

_____

FORGIVE ME FOR:

_____

_____

_____

_____

People To Pray For

HELP ME TO SHOW LOVE TODAY BY:

_____

_____

On My Mind

Tell God about your worries and/or desires.

. . . .

God, I give all my worries, fears, and desires to you. Please help me to trust you today.

. . . .

B

READ "I have told you these things, so that in me you may have peace. In this world you will have trouble. But take heart! I have overcome the world."

- John 16:33

— *Listen* —

What do you think God is saying in this Bible passage?

PRAY

ASK GOD TO GIVE YOU PEACE EVEN WHEN THE WORLD FEELS SCARY AND TO REMEMBER THAT HE IS STRONGER THAN ANY PROBLEM IN THE WORLD.

WONDER Have you ever heard something in the news that made you feel scared?

_____

_____

_____

_____

THANK-YOU FOR:

_____
_____
_____
_____

FORGIVE ME FOR:

_____
_____
_____
_____

On My Mind

Tell God about your
worries and/or desires.

People To Pray For

God, I give all my
worries, fears, and
desires to you.
Please help me to
trust you today.

HELP ME TO SHOW LOVE TODAY BY:

_____
_____

YOUR THOUGHTS MATTER!

• • • • • • • • • • • • • • • • • •

Did you enjoy using this prayer journal? Would you like to help other kids enjoy it too?

This is a small family-run business and we could use **your help** in spreading the word about our PB & J Journals! We would love to have you leave a great review wherever you purchased this journal. (Just be sure to ask your parents first.)

And I'd be happy to hear from you too! You can reach me at:

amy@morelikegrace.com

HOW ABOUT SOME FREEBIES?

Ask a Parent to Help You Explore These **Free** Printable Resources For Your Whole Family!

- Nature Scripture Scavenger Hunt
- Choose Your Own Adventure
  Bible-Reading Plan
- Scripture Prayer Cards for Kids
- Lunchbox Notes
- "Least of These" Family Prayer Chain
- *And many, many more!*

AVAILABLE AT WWW.MORELIKEGRACE.COM
(LOOK UNDER "FREE PRINTABLES")

MORE GREAT WAYS TO
GROW IN YOUR FAITH!

PB & J Prayer Journals

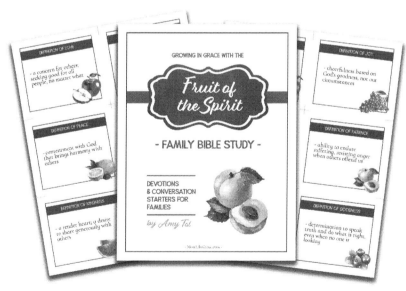

Fruit of the Spirit Bible Study

Made in the USA
Monee, IL
12 May 2022